# Goes Well With Beer

## Poetry and What-not

By
Erin J. Jones

Copyright © 2020 by Erin J. Jones
All Rights Reserved

No part of this publication may be reproduced, distributed, or transmitted in any form or by any means, including photocopying, recording, or other electronic or mechanical methods, without the prior written permission of the publisher, except in the case of brief quotations embodied in critical reviews and certain other noncommercial uses permitted by copyright law.

*For the beer enthusiasts and collectors that
make life worthwhile*

# Stumble Forward

When I was young, I was told that a good hobby would help me build character. Since I wanted to be a character when I grew up, I choose beer can collecting as a hobby. As I grew, my love for the hobby and all things beer grew. Through my hobby, I have had a chance to travel and meet people from all walks of life. It has also given me a chance to study history. As well as a chance to try new beers.

My love for writing and the written word came about the same time as my love for beer. I joined a local poetry group and the members did enjoy my beer related poetry. That is when my two interests collided and the seeds of this endeavor sprouted.

*Work is the curse of the drinking class*

– Oscar Wilde

# Table of Contents

Four A.M. .................................................................................. 1
Untitled .................................................................................... 2
Beer .......................................................................................... 4
Ninkasi ..................................................................................... 5
Phobias .................................................................................... 6
Butt Load ................................................................................. 7
Beer is the Foundation of Civilization ........................................ 8
An Ode to the B.C.C.A.* .......................................................... 9
Found in the Advertisements .................................................. 10
The Story of Carrie Nation ..................................................... 11
Saith Carrie Nation ................................................................ 14
Untitle .................................................................................... 16
Tiplings .................................................................................. 17
Beer Holidays ......................................................................... 19
Untitled .................................................................................. 22
Untitled .................................................................................. 23
To Pour .................................................................................. 24
Untitled .................................................................................. 25
Latest Love ............................................................................. 26
Dig The New Breed ................................................................ 27
Drink Me a Forty ................................................................... 28
Proof ...................................................................................... 31
What Ben Franklin Said ......................................................... 32
Well-dressed gentlemen .......................................................... 34
Protest .................................................................................... 37
Untitled .................................................................................. 38
Das Boot ................................................................................ 39

| | |
|---|---|
| These Old Friends | 40 |
| Untitled | 42 |
| Microbrew Logic | 43 |
| Untitled | 44 |
| Before Your Leisure | 45 |
| Untitled | 46 |
| Occupational Hazards | 47 |
| Untitled | 48 |
| Prohibition | 50 |
| Repeal | 51 |
| The First Beer Can | 53 |
| Reinheitsgebot | 54 |
| 56 Degrees | 55 |
| Untitled | 56 |
| Mothers Against Drunk Drivers | 58 |
| Yes, We Want No Billy Beer | 59 |
| Taking Flight | 60 |
| Appearance | 61 |
| Aroma | 62 |
| Taste | 63 |
| Mouth-feel | 65 |
| Finish | 65 |
| Drink Your Milk | 68 |
| Free Beer | 69 |
| Continuing Education | 70 |
| Quotable Quotes That We Like To Quote | 71 |
| Need Help, Wish to help | 86 |
| For the Collectors | 87 |
| Untitled | 89 |
| About The Author | 90 |

# Four A.M.

(One)
The room was as dark as Guinness
and cooled to the perfect cellar temperature.
Hypnos was just a tease
taking me to the edge just to deny me.
Oneiroi did not stop by to visit.
Meanwhile, Hermes showed old photographs
and told stories of long forgotten mishaps.

(Two)
The room was as cold as an Irish stout
and just as dark.
A clock ticked steadily
like the tapping of a funeral drum.
Meanwhile, a computer ran amuck,
randomly accessing files long thought to be deleted.

(Three)
Darkness poured into the room
like porter into a pint glass.
All was calm, quiet.
My muse refused to say good-night
or sing a lullaby.
And the voices in my head
told stories and lies about me.

## **Untitled**

I could never be a beer snob
It is just not my style
I see no point in limiting myself
I will try any beer once
some a dozen times,
maybe more…
It doesn't matter
Macro-brewed, craft-brewed
cold beer, cheap beer
If you enjoy it- enjoy it


*There is no such thing as bad beer. It's just that some taste better than others.*

– Billy Carter

GOES WELL WITH BEER

## Beer

The blue and red lights flash beer
And the walls of the house beer
Disneyland is for fools
All roads lead to beer
I have never married and they do not understand
she was the one who said beer
People like to tell me stories about their beer
The book beer reads beer
Sunny beer beach beer
This old town new beer
The pretty lass smiles beer
and the fishermen beer as well
In St. Louis we will beer
and beer some more
as we so often beer
craft shows craft beer
I am at a loss for beer
What more can I beer

## Ninkasi

Sumerian Goddess
the brewer and beer itself
*You who fills my mouth so full*
your devoted followers
sing their Hymn to You

Let the ladies do their graceful work
Set the malt to the ground
On large reed mats
spread the cooked mash
Coolness overcomes
And cast bread upon flowing waters
brewing it with honey and date
Soak the malt in a jar
Waves rise, waves fall
Noble dogs keep potentates away
The filtering vat
makes a pleasant sound

## Phobias

Zythophobia is the fear of beer.

Dipsophobia is the fear of drinking.

Methyphobia and Potophobia are the fear of alcohol.

Tavernapobia is the fear of going to a bar.

Zymocenosilicaphobia and Cenosillicaphobia are both the fear of an empty beer glass.

Oenophobia is the fear of wine.


I could find no specific mention of whisky, gin, or brandy.

## Butt Load

The actual definition

of

a butt load

is

108 imperial gallons

of ale.

True story.

# Beer is the Foundation of Civilization

Beer is the foundation of civilization
We stopped our nomadic ways to raise grains
We built farms and cities
We diversified our crops and brewed our yield
We stopped our nomadic ways to raise grains
We built farms and cities
And in the cities we find pubs
In the pubs friends gather
Beer is the language of friendship in many cultures
Beer is the way men bond as brothers
Beer is the foundation of civilization
We stopped our nomadic ways to raise our grains
We diversified our crops and brewed our yield
We built farms and cities
Beer is the foundation of civilization

## An Ode to the B.C.C.A.*

Beer can collectors are an odd lot
The only nuts in the world
Who have found other nuts to drink and trade with
They cannot distinguish between trash and treasure
An old, rusty can dug out of an old campsite
Has a place on a shelf in the home museum
Old dogs and old breweriana often find a good home
Oh sure, they are sociable and laugh heartily
And of course, they gather pieces of history
And write books on our brewing heritage to save for posterity
The walls of their homes are a mosaic of color
*The DIYer down the street does not understand*
*The walls are not a shade of beige*
*As they do on HGTV*
At the end of their days
Their friends will bottom open something cold and frothy
And toast life and friendship

*\*Brewery Collectibles Club of America originally known as Beer Can Collectors of America*

# Found in the Advertisements

The choicest product of the brewer's art
Finest beer you ever tasted
The finest beer in town
The original and genuine
Born of natural ingredients
Served cold in bottles
Perfect brewing water makes the perfect beer

Life is too short to drink cheap beer
Life is meant to be wild
Unleash the beast
Live the highlife
Go for the gusto

# The Story of Carrie Nation

June 5, 1900
With religious zeal
And a family history
of mental instability
She awakened to a
murmuring, singing voice
*Go to Kiowa*
*Take something in your hand*
*Throw at these places in Kiowa*
*And smash them*

June 7, 1900
She entered Dobson's Saloon
*Men, I have come to save you*
*from a drunkard's fate*
and gave the place
a damn good smashing

After a raid in Wichita
her husband joked
that she should take
a hatchet the next time
*That is the most sensible*
*thing you have said*
*since I married you*
The couple divorced
A legend was born

She was ready to
Carry A. Nation to Prohibition

Alone or accompanied by
hymn-singing women
she would march, sing, and pray
and be arrested 30 times
for "hatchetations"
The fines paid
by lecture tour fees
and the sales of souvenir hatchets

In Kansas's first steps
towards diversity
the signs would read
*All nations are welcome*
*except Carrie*

She published *The Hatchet*
and *The Smasher's Mail*
On Vaudeville
it did not sell
Her sermonizing was
not good comedy

She built Hatchet Hall
in Eureka Springs
and continued to let
the message ring

She fell ill one summer day
and where her mortal remains lay
stands a stone in tribute
*Faithful to the Cause of Prohibition,*
*She done what she could*

She did not
live to see
Prohibition
or its history

# Saith Carrie Nation

*God is a politician;*
    *so is the devil*
*Men are nicotine soaked,*
    *beer besmirched,*
        *whiskey greased,*
            *red-eyed devils*
*If you don't do it,*
    *then the women of this state will do it...*
        *You refused me the right to vote*
            *and I had to use a rock*
*Oh, I tell you, ladies,*
    *you never know what joy it gives you*
        *to start out to smash a rum shop*
*I felt invincible.*
    *My strength was that of a giant.*
        *God was certainly standing by me.*
            *I smashed five saloons with rocks*
                *before I ever took a hatchet*

*I believe in being everlasting on the warpath*

## **Untitled**

The hero saved the girl
but beer saved the world

Cavemen gathered grain
then it rained
again it rained
and our ancestors attained
something frothy and pure
the discovery of beer

In Mesopotamia
they laid the foundation
for civilization
to domesticate the grain
and to maintain
something so dear
a dependable supply of beer

*This is all thousands of years old. It's the same the world over. Anyone who has ever walked upright has loved beer, celebrated over it, told talks over it, hatched plots over it, courted over it. It's what we do as a species. It's what makes us human. We brew.*

– Allen Eames, Beer Anthropologist

## **Tiplings**

Tipling; the origin of the toast

>The King splashes wine
>>Into a taster's glass
>>>Does he die
>>>>Or does it pass?

Bock, so dark and bold
tell us the story
of the goat

Indian Pale Ale
my hoppy friend
soldier on until the end

Raddler
always a good reason
to go ride

Irish stout
thick and dark
Irish blessings
on Saint Patrick's Day

The most seasonal of beer
is an oddity called pumpkin beer
Too much pumpkin spice
for this man's pie

Thirty-three blended into one
and Blue Ribbons won
PBR me, baby

Champagne of Beer
Lady on the Moon
gives a toast

drank some damn good beer
met some damn good people
while micro-grooving

The Black and Tan
is an American thing
that the British
neither understand
nor wish to know

this cold amber ale
its bubbles dancing upwards
forming a good head

# **Beer Holidays**

January 1 - Hangover Day

January 24 - Beer Can Appreciation Day

February 24 - World Bartender Day

April 6 - New Beers Eve

April 7 - New Beers Day

April 11 - King Gambrinus Day

April 17 - Saison Day

April 23 - German Beer Day

May 7 - National Home-Brew Day

July 3 - National Independent Beer Run Day

July 8 - Saint Arnold's Day

August 1 - IPA Day

August 2 - International Beer Day

September 7 - National Beer Lover's Day

September 20 - Sour Beer Day

September 28 - Drink Beer Day

October 9 - Beer and Pizza Day

October 14 - Home-brewing Legalization Day

October 27 - National American Beer Day

November 3 - Learn to Homebrew Day

November 7 - International Stout Day

December 5 - Repeal Day (U.S.)

December 10 - National Lager Day

# Untitled

Did you not hear
of the cheer, served
so near to here

These pubs they brew
beer or two, that
is new and dear

I should say fresh
that is best, I
digress and cheers


*Sometimes too much drink is barely enough.*

– Mark Twain

## Untitled

To sample some good craft brew - pick four beers for flight
Sample each from light to dark - take time to enjoy
And let the flavors linger - each tells a story
If you wish for more in-depth-order a good pint


*A fine beer may be judged with only one sip, but it's better to be thoroughly sure.*

– Bohemian Proverb

# To Pour

**An Ale**
Gentle, steady
down a tilted glass
Steepen the angle
to avoid being flat
Just enough head
to give it a finger

**A Stout**
Pour your stout slowly
in two stages
for a creamier, solid head
that suit coffee-ish flavors

**A Hefeweizen**
Belgians wet the glass
before the gentle pour
The last few drops are rolled
yeast sediment loosen
Making the beer chosen
properly cloudy as we adore

## Untitled

Let us drink a beer
and have a bit of cheer
now that the work days done
time to have some fun

Let us drink some ale
and tell us the tell
of the one that got away
on your last sick day

## Latest Love

The bartender introduced me
 to a lovely blonde
She was everything
that I had dreamed
Her body was full
and seemed to dance
Her soft golden features
shined like diamonds
beneath the neon lights
She was smooth
and went down easy
My time with her
was pure pleasure
In the end
she was gone
leaving me
to desire another

## Dig The New Breed

*Are you thirsty for something different?*
*You may wish to try...*

Depravity Imperial Peanut Butter Stout
Red Brick Devine Bovine Chai Tea Milk Stout
80 Acres Hoppy Wheat
Chocolate Sombrero Chocolate Stout
Old Leghumper
Bourbon Double Cream Stout
Fresh As Helles
Pink Vapor Stew
Space Goat Pale Ale
Sticky Toffee Pudding Ale
Adios Pantalones

*And yes, these are real beers.*

# Drink Me a Forty

The trees swayed in the night air. I sat on a park bench, relaxing and watching them. Breathing deep, I could smell the rain smell in the air. I have always loved that smell. There is something refreshing about it, so pure and so simple.

I was feeling restless. This was the first warm spell of spring. The robins had returned and the flowers and the dogwood trees were in full bloom. Yet I had not had the time to enjoy them. My days had been spent at my work station, facing a computer screen, and enclosed on three sides by a cubicle. All of this was further enclosed by four rather drab office walls.

I moved from building to car and from car to building with nothing but a tease of sunshine to sustain me. I had a form of cabin fever, or Spring fever, or maybe it was a malady that should be called cubicle fever.

It was Friday evening, the work week was over. I just wanted to take a long walk, stretch my legs, and breathe some fresh air. Maybe head down to the liquor store and get a forty ounce bottle of something cold to wash away the work week with.

The weather forecast called for a twenty-five percent chance of rain that evening with a possibility of thunderstorms. The meteorologists on the local news made it sound like it could get bad, but they tend to overdramatize and most of the locals never worry until they hear the sirens or it gets severe enough for the local television stations to interrupt its commercials.

The weather was frustrating. Still, I had a vehicle two

blocks away if I really wanted to go. I breathed deep and relaxed, breathed deep that rain smell. I knew my decision before I made it. Something primal in me laughed, something youthful in me cheered. A smile crossed my face. My rising from the bench seemed more of a reaction than an action. My feet were moving towards their destination. I had to laugh at myself. It had been a long time since I had done anything foolish and high time that I did.

Children play in the rain. Ducks play in the rain. Sports are played in the rain. We spend large amount of money on therapy and seminars, trying to understand and touch our inner child. Yet we sit within the comforts of shelter to avoid the rain, snow, and the sunshine. We rarely take time to enjoy them.

I walked at a lively pace. The night air was refreshing. I saw lightning off in the distance. I was a block away from the store when a drop of rain hit my nose. I walked on. Another drop hit my cheek. One hundred feet from the door, it started up as a steady spring shower.

Stepping into the store, I viewed my options, and selected my beverage of choice. With purchase in hand, I stepped back outside, into the rain. The tempo of it picked up slightly as I crossed the street. I continued on unconcerned. Half way home, the storm opened up in earnest. Thunder roared and lightning flashed. A cold, hard, driving rain soaked me to the bone. I trudged on as cars passed by.

I walked down the street. Two neighbors, a man and wife sitting in chairs on their front porch, waved as I walked by. I waved back in a friendly manner. It was good to be smart enough not to come in out of the rain.

I made it back home soaked, cold, tired, and very much alive. I took a seat on the stoop at the front door of my apartment, sitting under the overhang of the roof, and popped the top on my forty. I watched the lightning dance in the distance. I relaxed and listened to the sound of the rain.

## **Proof**

Ben Franklin is misquoted, true
he spoke of wine
with the line

Beer is proof that God loves you
and wishes he
for you to be happy

But why argue history
when we have beer
and chance cheer
the end of the work day's misery

# What Ben Franklin Said

*Behold the rain*
*which descends from heaven*
*upon our vineyards;*
*there it enters the roots*
*of the vine,*
*to be changed into wine;*
*a constant proof*
*that God loves us,*
*and loves to see us happy*

From a 1779 letter to Abbe Morellet

# Well-dressed gentlemen

The proper beer
in the proper glass
Serve it right
or let it pass
per Belgian protocol

If you are in your pints
shakers, nonics, and imperials
will not fail
for porter, stouts, and ales

The stemmed trio
chalice, tulip, and snifter
allow complex flavours
and aromas
to be savoured

Pilsner and Weissbier
so tall and narrow
show the body in good light
and supports a fine head

Their cousin, strange,
the word a name
for a German pole
will take a kolsh
to the nose

GOES WELL WITH BEER

Tankard, krug, and stein
will work just fine
for traditional ale and bier
from England or the Rhine

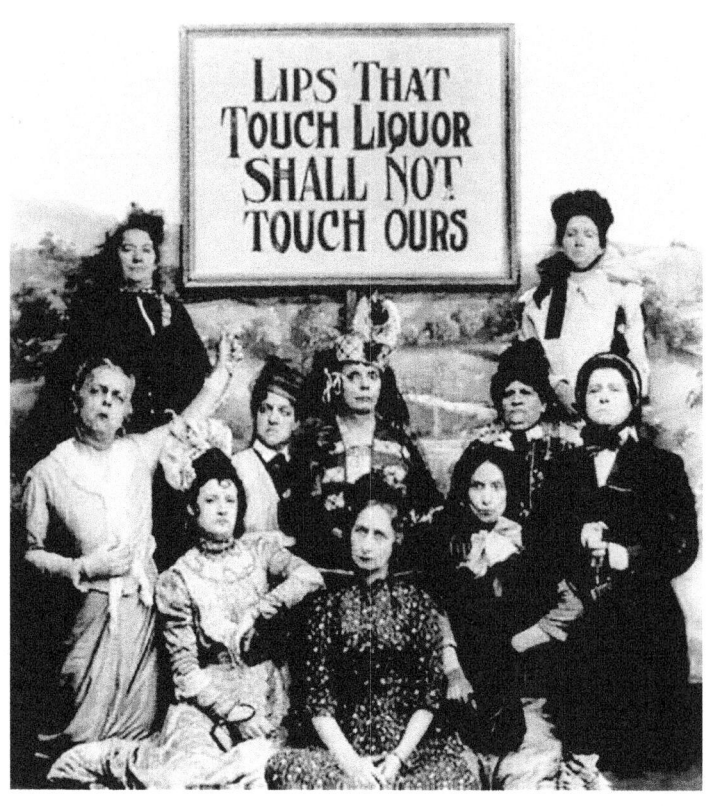

## Protest

*Lips that touch liquor*
*Shall not touch ours*
read the sign
bold and clear
With sober eye
I looked upon
the ladies there
and opted for beer

## Untitled

**A**ll
**B**eer
**c**onnoisseurs
**D**rink
**E**very
**F**rothy
**G**oodness
**H**e encounters
**I**mbibing on
**J**ovial
**K**olsches and
**L**imitless
**M**eads
**N**ever
**O**verly
**P**essimistic or
**Q**uestioning
**R**eal
**S**eriously
**T**he
**U**ltimate
**V**alue of the
**W**ort
**(e)X**periments of
**Y**our local
**Z**ymologist

## Das Boot

A Prussian General proclaimed
if his soldiers attained
victory on the battlefield
he would give a grand salute
and drink his bier from his boot
The day was won victorious

With quick decision
he did commission
a large glass in the shape of his boot
And this rendition
has become a tradition
in Deutschland even today

See if you can wield
and not a drop spill
a good drink of fine German bier
Don't forget to flick the glass
before you clockwise pass
and wish the next person good luck

*It takes beer to make thirst worthwhile.*

– German Proverb

## These Old Friends

**Water**
*It's the water*
said Olympia Brewing
Cold, pure, artesian
at ninety-two percent
it carries a heavy weight

**Wort**
These lovely cracked grains
lautering in a hot bath
convert starch to sugar
add bittering hops to flavor
and pitch it when it is cool

**Hops**
The cone shaped flower
this humulus lupulus
its essential oils
add bitterness and preserve
and give beauty to the beer

**Yeast**
Once an unknown
this funky living fungi
eats sugar in the wort
eating all that it can take
leaving alcohol in its wake

**Fermentation**
Mother always said
*Good things come to those who wait*
How long should good take
fifteen, forty-five, or more
good brew is worth waiting for

## Untitled

The workers who built the pyramids
took their wages in beer-
one gallon per day-
Not bad work if you could get it

The Roman Legionnaires
who conquered all of the known world
took their pay in salt

## Microbrew Logic

I grew up in the American beer wastelands
Our lagers were thin, weak, and pale
far from England's robust ales
Macro-brewing; the art of the business man
water, yeast, and adjuncts in a can
But history will tell the tale
of how we learned to appreciate a quality ale
when micro-breweries came to stand

What we have is not new
though we once went eschew
Our founding fathers drank in pubs
that brewed their own beer and cooked up grub
If one learns, one will see
brewpubs are heritage and history

## Untitled

the spring rains and summer sun
nurture the seed and the soil
hop flowers go to harvest
good beer they become


*From man's sweat and God's love, beer came into the world.*

– Saint Arnoldus, Patron Saint of Hop-Pickers

# Before Your Leisure

brewing remains
      hard, physical work
           long hours
                  not-always-glamorous
shoveling wet malt
      scrubbing drains
           hosing out kegs

fermentation
      tasting
           waiting
                anticipating
finally
      the
           first
                pour

# Untitled

There is a brewpub in Nantucket
where patrons quaff ale by the bucket
A sin not to share
such quality beer
Put it in a can and truck it


*I feel sorry for people who don't drink. When they wake up in the morning, that's as good as they're going to feel all day.*

– Frank Sinatra

## Occupational Hazards

There is an old joke
that goes:

A brewery worker died
after he fell into the vat
of beer
and drowned

*Please tell me he did not suffer*
cried his distraught widow

*Not very much*
said the plant manager
*but he did climb out*
*three times to pee*

## Untitled

Brew master Arthur Guinness
was Ireland's greatest genius
and the genesis of Irish stout
Irish eyes smiling and laughter
with a good pint of Liffey water
on Saint Paddy' Day give a shout

*He that drinketh strong beer and goes to bed right mellow, lives as he ought to live and dies a hearty fellow.*

– Anonymous

GOES WELL WITH BEER

# Prohibition

The Temperance movement began in the early 1800's, many believing that alcohol was to blame for society's ills. Intoxication was blamed for all sorts of crimes, debauchery, and evil. Organizations such as the Women's Christian Temperance Movement and the Anti-Saloon League worked to dissuade people from becoming intoxicated at first, before their focus turned to complete prohibition of alcohol consumption.

In 1919 the 18th Amendment was ratified, prohibiting the sale and manufacture of alcohol. It went into effect on January 16, 1920. The Volstead Act was passed on October 28, 1919 to clarify the law concerning "beer, wine, or other intoxicating malt or vinous liquors". It also set specific fines and jail terms for violations. The period known as Prohibitions, and sometimes called the Great Experiment, had begun.

Prohibition is the reason the Roaring Twenties roared. This was the decade of gangsters, bathtub gin, and speakeasies. Rumrunners brought rum from the Caribbean, and gangsters brought whiskey in from Canada. Down South, moonshiners distilled illegal whisky in the moonlight and bootleggers modified their cars to outrun the "revenuers". These modifications were the origin of NASCAR.

*"During Prohibition it was said that tailors would ask customers what size pockets they wanted, pint or quart."*

*– Will Rogers*

# Repeal

Prohibition lasted thirteen years. On March 23, 1933 President Franklin D. Roosevelt, signed the Cullen-Harrison Act, which made it legal to manufacture certain alcoholic products. December 5, 1933 the 21st Amendment is ratified by Congress, making the 18th Amendment the first and only amendment to the U.S. Constitution to be repealed. At 12:01A.M. on Friday, April 7 beer became legal again in the United States. Across the nation, the thirsty raised a toast.

*This would be a good time for a beer.*

– Franklin D. Roosevelt upon signing The Cullen-Harrison Act

# The First Beer Can

The American Can Company had begun experimenting with canned beer in 1909. However, the cans could not withstand the pressure caused by carbonation, up to eighty pounds per square inch, and they would explode. The cans that did not explode had a metallic taste to the beer that was very reminiscent of canned orange juice. This problem was later solved when the company developed "keg-lining" by using a moldable plastic called vinylite to coat the inside of the can.

Development was put on hold as beer production stopped during prohibition. When prohibition ended and the surviving breweries were scrambling to get beer back into production and back in the market, research and development of the beer can began in earnest once again. The American Can Company went to The Gottfried Krueger Brewing Company in Newark, NJ with a proposal to build a canning line and pay for the initial test batches if Kruger would submit their beer to the can test.

On January 24, 1935 Krueger's Cream Ale became the first beer in a can to be sold to the public and the public gave it a 91 percent approval rating.

# Reinheitsgebot

In 1516 Duke Wilhelm IV of Bavaria wrote the first consumer protection law known as Reineitsgebot. It stated that true Bavarian beer could be made with nothing other than malted barley or wheat, hops and water. It was updated later to include yeast which had not been discovered when the law was written. This law dealt with pricing structure as well.

*Life is too short to drink bad beer.*

– Anonymous

## 56 Degrees

Room temperature is a misnomer
my good Feller
Ales and wine are best served
the temperature of the cellar

## **Untitled**

This stein
holds memories
good beer
good friends
and laughs
that have passed

The brewery no longer
produces the golden brew
but its stein still stands
as witness
in its place
on the collector's shelf

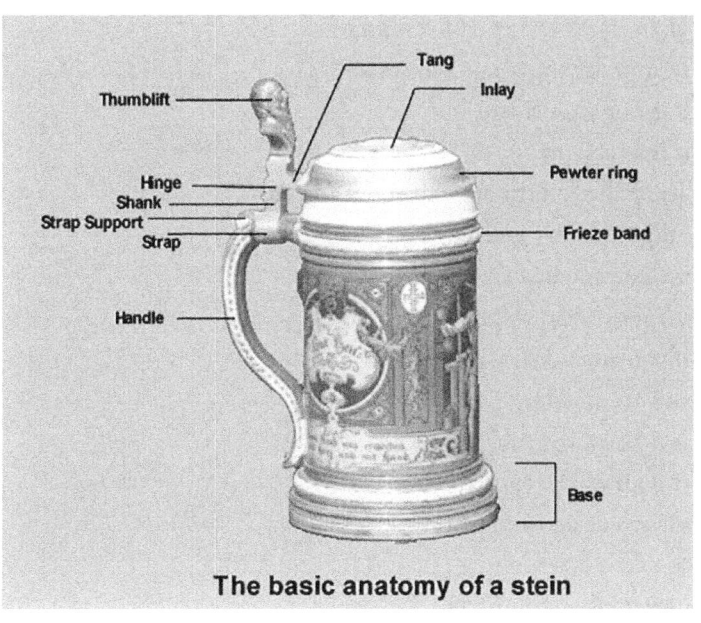

The basic anatomy of a stein

# Mothers Against Drunk Drivers

Mothers Against Drunk Drivers
are MADD for a damn good reason
There are no acceptable excuses
Drunk driving is not a mistake
It is not an accident
It is a fuck up
The police on the street can tell you that
Judge and jury will agree
the paramedic may tell you
the mortician will have no chance
If you are old enough to drink
you are an adult
you know the rules
you know the consequences
Have a designated driver
or take a taxi
Never take a foolish chance

## Yes, We Want No Billy Beer

In all my years
I have yet to hear
a collector say
they wanted Billy Beer
Madison Avenue be damned!
The marketing was but a scam!
Collectors determine the value of the cans
Price is driven by scarcity and desirability
You don't need an economics degree to understand
when supply far exceeds demand
there is no value in the can

Yes, we want no Billy Beer

# Taking Flight

In 2017, there was an estimated 2,252 brew pubs operating in the United States. By the end of 2018 that number had surpassed the 7,000 mark and growing. A trip to any local brewery will show that more and more people are discovering the joy of "fresh-brewed" beer every day. The offerings vary from mild to wild, old standards to extreme innovations.

I have yet to find a beer that was not worth trying at least once. Many beers I have tried have become favorites and beer I drink on regular basis. Some were interesting, but not something that I wanted to have more of.

When you are trying a new beer or visiting a brew pub, do not just chug, gulp, or quaff the beer. It is best to take some time to fully enjoy and appreciate what you are drinking.

The following are some pointers for sampling flights or mix-and-match six packs. Beer tasting does not have to be pretentious as wine tasting, but many of the same rules apply. These rules are basic, imperfect rules of thumb. If you wish, you can Google and learn more about beer tasting on our friend the internet.

> local beer
> local business
> your neighbor's art

## **Appearance**

When you pour your beer into a glass, the first thing you will probably notice is its appearance. Of course, the glass should be clear for the viewing. Hold the beer up to the light and notice its color and whether it is clear or cloudy. Note the color of the head and the beer's head retention. Color, per se, does not determine the quality of the beer. The lighter the color- the lighter tasting the beer is an imperfect rule of thumb. Likewise, the darker the beer- the stronger the taste. Most people go from the lightest color to the darkest when sampling a flight of beer.

If by chance you see bubbles sticking to the side of the glass; that is a sign of a improperly washed beer glass. A lot of beer enthusiasts soak their beer glasses in bleach water before cleaning and wash them separate from other dishes. Extra work I know, but good beer is worth it.

six in a row
move from light to dark
sample each one's kiss

# Aroma

Olfaction (that is a fancy word for the sense of smell) accounts for up to 90 to 95% of your ability to taste (that is the reason children hold their noses when eating weird green vegetables). Breathe in with your nose once or twice and then breathe in through your open mouth for full olfactory experience. What do you smell? Light beers smell more of hops and dark beers smell more of barley and chocolate, and even coffee. Ales tend to have a fruitiness from their yeast.

> Give your beer a nose
> as you would a rose
> or a fine perfume

## **Taste**

Of course, everybody's favorite part is tasting the beer. Resist the temptation to gulp it down. Take a few seconds to swirl it around to all parts of your mouth. Let it linger and notice the different flavors. Beer can be surprisingly complex in taste.

>savor the flavor
>let it linger
>for the moment

## **Mouth-feel**

Mouthfeel is simply how the beer feels physically on your tongue (I know, self-explanatory, right?). This is an important character of beer. Does it feel thin, thick, or fizzy?

> Belgian lace
> in the empty glass
> tells a story

## **Finish**

Take pause after a ship. Observe the aftertaste. Does in disappear or linger? Sweet or bitter? What flavors remain? Does it invite you to take another sip? It should be noted, that unlike wine that is spit out after tasting, beer must be swallowed in order to taste the hop bitterness on the back of the tongue.

> Oh what fun!
> hops dancing
> on the tongue

# **Impression**

Once all is said and done and the glass sits empty; what is your impression of the experience from pour to the last aftertaste? Was it good? Was the body and flavor pleasing? Or did you find it disappointing? Would you order it again or chance to meet a new friend?

>   an empty glass
>   the bottom reflecting
>   what has passed

GOES WELL WITH BEER

## **Drink Your Milk**

In a container of horse hide
Joggled over a long days ride
This fermented mare's milk, kumis
Will end your day with a soft kiss

## Free Beer

Free beer tomorrow
the sign does say

But today
becomes yesterday

and right now
is always today

The elusive tomorrow
remains hours away

# Continuing Education

You have discovered a love for beer
Where do you go from here?
Education is always dear
Do more than drink the draft
take time to learn of the craft
If you ask you local brewer
he may offer you a tour
and show you how beer is made
And it is always right
to sample flights
to learn what you enjoy
You can study history
on Google and other media
But most important
be sincere
when you speak of beer
There is something to be said
about anything
that one truly appreciates

# Quotable Quotes That We Like To Quote

"Ah, good ol' trustworthy beer. My love for you will never die."

– Homer Simpson

"There is an ancient Celtic axiom that says 'Good people drink good beer.' Which is true, then as now. Just look around you in any public barroom and you will quickly see: Bad people drink bad beer. Think about it."

– Hunter S. Thompson

"If you ever reach total enlightenment while drinking beer, I bet it makes beer shoot out your nose."

– Jack Handey

"I've read that the ancient Chinese art of feng shui can bring a sense of peace, well-being, and positive energy to a home - same as beer."

– W. Bruce Cameron

"What I like about beer is that you basically just drink it, and then you order another one. You don't sniff at it, or hold it up to the light and slosh it around, and above all you don't drone on and on about it, the way people do with wine. Your beer drinker tends to be a straightforward, decent, friendly, down-to-earth person…"

– Dave Barry

"Alcohol is necessary for a man so that he can have a good opinion of himself, undisturbed by the facts."

– Finley Peter Dunne

"To alcohol! The cause of - and solution to - all of life's problems!"

– Homer Simpson

"Some people wanted Champagne and caviar when they should have had beer and hot dogs."

– Dwight D. Eisenhower, U.S. President

"For we could not now take time for further search or consideration (to land our ship), our victuals being much spent, especially our Beere."

– Ship's log of The Mayflower

"I don't have a drinking problem, expect when I can't get a drink."

– Tom Waits

"If God had wanted us to filter our beer, he wouldn't have given us livers."

– Larry Bell, Bell's Brewery

"You can do anything with beer that you can do with wine. Beer is great for basting and marinating meat and fish."

– Grant Wood

"Fermentation and civilization are inseparable."

— John Ciardi

"When the bee comes to your house, let her have beer: you may wish to visit the bee's house someday."

— Congolese Proverb

"Always do sober what you said you'd do drunk. That'll teach you to keep your mouth shut."

— Ernest Hemingway

"Beer will get you through times of no money better than money will get you through times of no beer."

— Freddie Freak

"There is nothing in the world like the first taste of beer."

— John Steinbeck

"An alcoholic is someone you don't like who drinks just as much as you do."

— Dylan Thomas

"Beer it's the best damn drink in the world."

— Jack Nicholson

"Fermentation may have been a greater discovery than fire."

— David Rains Wallace

"An oppressive government is more to be feared than a tiger, or a beer."

– Confucius

"Milk is for babies. When you grow up you have to drink beer."

– Arnold Schwarzenegger

"Beer makes you feel the way you ought to feel without beer."

– Henry Lawson

"I fear the man who drinks water and so remembers this morning what the rest of us said last night."

–Greek Proverb

"I know a man who gave up smoking, drinking, sex, and rich food. He was healthy right up to the day he killed himself."

– Johnny Carson

"Alcohol is a very necessary article...It enables Parliament to do things at eleven at night that no sane person would do at eleven in the morning."

– George Bernard Shaw

"Whiskey and beer are a man's worst enemies...but the man that runs away from his enemies is a coward!"

– Zeca Pagodinho

"There can't be good living where there is not good drinking."

– Ben Franklin

"All the best pubs are built on a hill, so you can slope in and roll out."

– Benny Bellamacina

"Better thin beer than an empty jug."

– Danish Proverb

"Nothing ever tasted better than a cold beer on a beautiful afternoon with nothing to look forward to but more of the same."

– Hugh Hood

"I drink to make other people interesting."

– George Jean Nathan

"Wherever beer is brewed, all is good - wherever beer is drunk, life is good."

– Czech Proverb

"You guys came by to have some fun. You'll come and stay all night, I fear. But I know how to make you run. I'll serve you all generic beer."

– Irish Toast

"Alcohol is like love. The first kiss is magic, the second is intimate, the third is routine. After that you take the girl's clothes off."

– Raymond Chandler

"People who don't drink are afraid of revealing themselves."

– Humphrey Bogart

"When I read about the evils of drinking, I gave up reading."

– Henny Youngman

"A little bit of beer is divine medicine."

– Paracelsus

"Stay busy, get plenty of exercise, and don't drink too much. Then again, don't drink too little."

– Herman Smith-Johannsen, cross-county skier

"I've only ever been in love with a beer bottle and a mirror."

– Sid Vicious

"Beer is an improvement on water itself."

– Grant Johnson

"I'm off for a quiet pint - followed by fifteen noisy ones."

– Gareth Chilcott

"Bad beer is like bad art - if you endure enough of it, eventually you forget the alternatives."

– Stephen Greenleaf

"My doctor told me to watch my drinking. Now I drink in front of a mirror."

– Rodney Dangerfield

"Beer is made by man, wine by God."

– Martin Luther

"Sobriety diminishes, discriminates, and says no; drunkenness expands, unites, and says yes."

– William James

"I'm gaining weight the right way. I'm drinking beer."

– Johnny Damon

"Beer is a wholesome liquor…it abounds with nourishment."

– Dr. Benjamin Rush

"I am very picky about my people and my beer."

– Shelby Lynne

"Why we are here: To tremble at the terrible beauty of the stars, to shed a tear at the perfection of Beethoven's symphonies, and to crack a cold one now and then."

– David Letterman

"Wine is but a single broth, ale is meat, drink, and cloth."

– English Proverb

"The tavern will compare favorably with the church."

– Henry David Thoreau

"History flows forward on rivers of beer."

– Anonymous

"Drunkenness does not create vice; it merely brings it into view."

– Seneca

"They who drink beer will think beer."

– Washington Irving

"A meal of bread, cheese and beer constitutes the perfect food."

–Queen Elizabeth 1

"Note to self: no matter how bad life gets, there's always beer."

– Norm Macdonald

"Would I were in an alehouse in London! I would give all my fame for a pot of ale and safety."

– William Shakespeare

"The first glass is for myself, the second for my friends, the third for good humor, and the fourth for my enemies."

– Sir William Temple

"Alcohol may be man's worst enemy, but the Bible says love your enemy.'

– Frank Sinatra

"Blessed is the mother who gives birth to a brewer."

– Czech saying

"Beer may not solve your problems, but neither will water or milk."

– Wiley

"Show me how you drink and I will tell you who you are."

– Emile Peynaud, Oenologist

"Beer drinkin' don't do half the harm of love makin.'"

– Old New England Proverb

"The worst thing about some men is that when they are not drunk they are sober."

– William Butler Yeats

"What I like about playing America is that you can be pretty sure that you're not going to get hit with a full can of beer when you're singing and I really enjoy that."

– Joe Strummer

"It's amazing how many times the words 'I need another drink' has bailed me out of awkward conversations."

– Unknown

"For thousands of years…women maintained power and status in male dominated societies through their skills as brewsters."

– Alan Eames, Beer Anthropologist

"Life, alas, is very drear. Up with the glass! Down with the beer!"

– Louis Untermeyer

"As he brews so shall he drink."

–Ben Johnson, playwright

"Any foreign trip is better if you can visit a few breweries."

–Fred Eckhardt

"I have a beer belly."

– Christy Turlington

"Without question, the greatest invention in the history of mankind is beer. Oh, I grant that the wheel was also a fine invention, but the wheel does not go nearly as well with pizza."

– Dave Barry

"I've never, ever tasted beer."

– Mike Huckabee

"You can't be a real country unless you have beer and an airline - it helps if you have some kind of football team, or some nuclear weapons, but at the very least you need a beer."

– Frank Zappa

"24 hours in a day, 24 beers in a case. Coincidence?"

– Stephen Wright

"The best audience is intelligent, well-educated, and a little drunk."

– Alben W. Barkley, Former U.S. Vice President

"The mouth of a perfectly happy man is filled with beer."

– Egyptian Proverb

"He who drinks beer sleeps well."

– Unknown German Monk

"In 1969, I gave up women and alcohol. It was the worst twenty minutes of my life."

– George Best

"I drink a lot of beer."

– Eric Bischoff

"Many battles have been fought and won by soldiers nourished on beer."

– Frederick the Great

"Beer is sacred business, a mood-altering food substance that may have preserved the human species. To drink beer is to be human."

– Alan Eames, Beer Anthropologist

"My first commercial was for Miller High Life Beer."

– Casey Kasem

"His was a great sin who first invented consciousness. Let us lose it for a few hours."

– F. Scott Fitzgerald

"Paintings are like beer, only beer tastes good and it is hard to stop drinking beer."

– Billy Carter

"Beer is the center of everything. Everything revolves around beer. When you drink, everything revolves. Therefore beer is the center of everything."

– University of Waterloo Engineers

"Prohibition makes you want to cry into your beer and denies you the beer to cry into."

– Don Marquis

"The church is near, but the road is icy. The bar is far away, but I will walk carefully."

– Russian Proverb

"Payday came and with it, beer."

– Rudyard Kipling

"God has a soft voice, as soft and full as beer."

– Anne Sexton

"Everybody should believe in something. I believe I'll have another drink."

– W.C. Fields

Beer - because one doesn't solve the world's problems over white wine."

– Anonymous

"I love football and beer and have a normal girlfriend."

– Josh Duhamel

"One drink is just right, two are too many, three too few."

– Spanish Proverb

"Beauty is in the eye of the beer holder."

– Kinky Friedman

"Beer, if drunk in moderation, softens the temper, cheers the spirit and promotes health."

–Thomas Jefferson

"Depth perception and beer obviously weren't related."

– Katie McGarry

"Beer is the reason we get up each afternoon."

– Ray McNeill

"Let no man thirst for good beer."

– Sam Adams

"A woman drove me to drink and I didn't even have the decency to thank her."

– W.C. Fields

"For a quart of Ale is a meal for a King."

– William Shakespeare

"Pretty women make us BUY beer. Ugly women make us DRINK beer."

– Al Bundy

"Every loaf of bread is a tragic story of grains that could've become beer, but didn't."

– Walter Thornburg

"You're not drunk if you can lie on the floor without holding on."

– Dean Martin

# Need Help, Wish to help

Alcoholic Anonymous

www.AA.org

Al-Anon

www.Al-Anon.org

Narcotics Anonymous

www.NA.org

Mothers Against Drunk Driving

www.MADD.org

## For the Collectors

Brewery Collectibles Club of America

www.bcca.com

National Association of Brewery Advertising

www.nababrew.com

American Breweriana Association

www.americanbreweriana.org

East Coast Breweriana Association

www.eastcoastbrew.com

Mobile Booking Cage

## Untitled

Please remember
      Never never
           Ever ever
                  Drink and drive

# About The Author

Erin J. Jones was born in Wisconsin and Raised in Arkansas. After surviving his small town upbringing, he went off the college, dropped out of college, and enlisted in the U.S. Army. After serving his country as a cavalry scout, he returned to the University of Arkansas and earned degrees in communication and economics. He started collecting beer cans and breweriana in 1976. He is a member of the Brewery Collectibles Club of America and attends local trade shows and CANventions when he can. He works as a mild-mannered salesman by day and a struggling writer at night.

*www.ErinJonesWriter.com*

# GOES WELL WITH BEER

Made in the USA
Monee, IL
26 July 2021